THE MOST UNLIKELY MILLIONAIRE

A Guide to Financial Freedom

Eric Shepard

Shepard Media
18941 Vista Real
Yorba Linda, CA 92886

ISBN: 0991260406
ISBN 13: 9780991260409

www.MostUnlikelyMillionaire.com

Printed in the United States of America

10 9 8 7 6 5 4 3 2 1

Disclaimer:

In this book, I discuss the blue ocean strategy, which W. Chan Kim and
Renee Mauborgne wrote about in their book, *BLUE OCEAN STRATEGY: How
to Create Uncontested Market Space and Make Competition Irrelevant*. I do
not wish to plagiarize their work or infringe on their copyright. I believe that
the blue ocean strategy is an important concept. I am simply sharing how
I used the strategy described by Kim and **Mauborgne** to turn my business
around.

DEDICATION

"They" say book dedications are an act of love. It is in this spirit that I dedicate this book to: my beautiful wife, Stacie, our four amazing children, Isabella, Antonio, Lorenzo and Francesca (aka Freshie).

I also want to thank Dan Blair and John Trail for their hard work and help building our business over the years. It's been quite the ride and I could not have done it without you guys.

And, no dedication would be complete without a shout out to Mom and Dad. Thank you all for your love and support.

CONTENTS

HOW THIS BOOK CAN HELP YOU

You have most likely heard of Bill Gates and Mark Zuckerberg—men who jumped from ordinary lives to super-stardom and wealth. But you probably don't see a connection between what they accomplished and what is possible for you.

This story is different.

This book is about an ordinary guy, with ordinary amounts of talent and intelligence, sharing a few things about his life, his business, and his success. In the following pages, I share concepts and *aha* moments that I discovered on my journey to becoming an unlikely millionaire.

I hope that these insights will help you improve your life, inspire you to create a business, and guide you to becoming an unlikely millionaire.

I want you to say, "If this guy can do it, I can do it, too."

This is not a get-rich-quick book. I think most of those lead to disappointment.

The truth is that most first-generation millionaires (people whose fathers or grandfathers did not hand them the millionaire baton) became rich by changing what they thought was possible in their lives, by taking a few risks, and by working pretty darned hard. In most cases, it took ten or more years to reach their current income level, satisfaction, and lifestyle.

If you think about it, we all work. So why not work in a way (maybe in a different career, or in your own business), which will produce grander and more satisfying results?

This idea was a game-changer for me. I was working eight to ten hours a day, investing my blood, sweat, and tears into someone else's business.

I started to ponder. I realizedthat I could actually take a different direction in my life. I saw a glimmer of hope and limitless possibilities. I imagined what the future could look like if I changed my direction and took control of my life.

I asked myself, if I am putting in the hours anyway, why not deposit the work and stress in a vehicle that, if done correctly, will turn my effort into gold for me someday?

This book is for people who are curious, and a little hungry, to discover what happened in the life of an average Joe, which propelled him from a life of struggling to make ends meet, into a very happy life with a beautiful wife, loving children, great health, and more money than he ever dreamed of.

This book is an inspirational guide to how you can improve your life by changing the way you think about your life.

I believe there are millions of people who have at least a twinge of curiosity, and who wonder if their lives could be better than they are now. They want to know if it is somehow possible to start their own business, to make better choices, and to live the life of their dreams.

What holds people back from being all they want to be?

In my life of living, loving, and learning, I have discovered a few things that prevent people from achieving total happiness. I want to share my life lessons with everyone who believes that there is something better out there for them. If the following thoughts have ever crossed your mind, this book is for you:

"Can I start my own business?" or "Can I work for an employer who appreciates me, and offers career advancement?"

"Can I make more money than I ever dreamed of?"

To those thoughts, I say yes. Yes, you can have the life of your dreams.

To realize your dreams, you have to do two things:

1. Have the courage to try something new.

2. Take action.

Ideas are nothing without action—but sometimes it is difficult to get out of your own way. All it takes is a shift in attitude, and a new way of thinking. In this book, I will show you how I did it.

Sometimes it feels like life keeps us in little boxes. I want to inspire you to get out of your box and reach for the stars. It is time to break out. It is time for you to step up and claim your greatness.

If I can do it, you can do it!

HOW DID I GET HERE?

It's 3:57 in the morning… Way too early to get out of bed. My plan was to sleep until at least 6:00 a.m. so I would have adequate rest before a much-anticipated family road trip. My family had been planning an RV adventure for months, and today was the day we were finally heading out. My excitement would not let me go back to sleep.

I laughed at myself… I was worse than the kids. Then I started to think about the kids' reaction when I pulled the new RV into the driveway yesterday. They were up and down, in and out, checking every little nook and cranny, "calling" beds, and deciding who was going to sleep where. Last night was the rare occasion when they needed no reminders to brush their teeth and get ready for bed—because in the morning, they were going on the trip of a lifetime.

Try as I might, I could not stop the wheels spinning in my head. I gave up and got out of bed… Might as well get this party started.

I got dressed and walked out to the driveway. As I stared at the gleaming, enormous RV with every upgraded feature, the thought occurred to me… Not only do I have a giant RV, but I also have a home that is not the normal three-bedroom, one-and-a-half-bath house. I have my dream home, with extra features that I never thought I would be able to afford—a detached garage, a workout room, and a beautiful office.

My thoughts shifted to my beautiful wife and all the hard work she put into getting ready for the trip—planning, pre-cooking, and trying her best to remember everything for everyone—and I thought about how lucky I was to have her.

A few minutes later, the kids came running outside, all on their best behavior, and raring to go. My oldest son, Antonio, walked directly up to me, gave me a big hug, and told me he loved me. He actually thanked me for the forthcoming RV trip.

Holy smokes! Can all four of these beautiful, well-adjusted, smart, and loving kids be mine?

It's funny how we get used to the things (nice things and not-so-nice things) that we have around us all the time. We seem to take so much for granted, but not on this day.

On this day, in the early morning chill and pre-sunrise shadows, it became clear to me that I have an amazing and wonderful life.

In my head, I heard a line from a Talking Heads song, "Bah bump... Is this my beautiful wife? Is this my beautiful house? How did I get here?"

I remember when I was struggling to eke out a living. All I wanted was to be able to buy my own house. I would have gladly settled for an average house with a postage-stamp sized yard.

If I had not changed my way of thinking, I am sure I would have been satisfied with a basic house, with few amenities. Look at what changing my thinking had done for me and my family!

In my early twenties, I felt a curiosity about what was possible for me. I was depressed, and broke, and had little hope for the future. I learned to have an open mind and imagined how my life could be better. My inner voice said, "It doesn't have to be like this."

I started listening to that inner voice. It was as if I had been asleep for twenty-some years and finally woke up to the fact that I could continue down the same road and get the same results—or I could change my thinking and create different results. I decided to look at my life from a different perspective. I felt a burning desire for change, created by a shift in my thinking.

Thoughts *do* become things.

If you *expect* your life to be mediocre, your life *will* be mediocre. If you expect your life to be full of abundance, your life will be full of abundance.

I am living proof of what is possible when you believe in yourself and know that you can have and achieve anything you set your mind to.

I will show you how.

3

HOW I BECAME THE MOST UNLIKELY MILLIONAIRE

My parents were very young when they started their family, and we had a middle-class lifestyle. I had a good childhood. I had many friends, and up until the seventh grade, I was popular and thought of myself in a good light. But from the seventh grade onward, I drifted into self-doubt, a lack of confidence, and regret.

I am not sure how or why the shift occurred. I do remember clearly feeling inadequate. I was happy and confident in middle school, but in high school, I lost sight of who I was.

I believed that I was not as good as other kids in most areas of life. I beat myself up for anything that went wrong. I started hanging out in the wrong places with the wrong crowd. I started drinking heavily and doing drugs.

I became depressed and out of touch with reality. At one point, after getting into trouble with my parents, I even considered suicide. I was home alone, and I remember crying while reaching into the medicine cabinet. Standing there, with the pills in my hand, I told myself that suicide was the right thing to do, but I could not get the courage to actually do it. I felt like a failure yet again.

I thought so little of myself; I could not imagine accomplishing great things. For example, my favorite coach from my Pop Warner football days was the assistant high school football coach. He asked me to join the high school football team. He asked twice, and I turned him down twice. He was surprised, since he had seen my talent and skill on the field for years. He seemed to think I would be great, but for reasons I still do not understand, I told him no. The "talking in my head" said that I was not up to it.

I cannot express the deep regret and disappointment I felt when I attended high school football games, sitting on a cold metal bench in the stands, and hearing the names of players who were celebrated as heroes and stars. I knew I was a better football player than most of my fellow classmates, because I had played with them for years in Pop Warner Football.

The truth is, I loved playing football and I was really good at it, but my mind got in the way. It created obstacles to keep me from doing something I loved to do and that I was good at.

Fortunately, later in life, I learned from many of my earlier mistakes and I broke free from my limited thinking.

I could sum up the challenges and disappointments I faced in high school as a typical teenage phase. Whatever the cause, I emerged from high school unready for the world. I had not yet figured out what I wanted to do with my life.

As a matter of fact, if we had voted for who was the most unlikely to become a millionaire (instead of the most likely to succeed or the class clown), I would have won. Then, I actually might have been popular for ten seconds in my miserable high school years.

I started to "wake up" when I enrolled in a local community college. When I was not attending classes, I worked 20-30 hours a week, and I was fortunate enough to get some financial assistance from my parents. This was a blessing, and I am grateful for their help and their desire to get me through college. After changing majors several times, I graduated from California State University, Fullerton when I was twenty-one, with a degree in communication.

The only job I could get right out of college was in sales, which I hated. I was shy and did not like talking to strangers. I took the job only because I needed to pay my bills. And, quite frankly, I did not think I had a choice. I didn't know at the time that I could do whatever I chose to do. I was clueless.

I was a starving college student, and I struggled even more after graduating. I clearly remember the time my mom came by for a surprise visit, just after I was out of college. She noticed that the nice wicker chair she had given me as a house-warming gift was missing.

She asked where it was, and I told her that I had to sell it to pay the rent. I felt so ashamed. She seemed to understand, but I could also see the worry in her eyes.

I remember a telephone conversation I had with my brother shortly after I graduated college. I mentioned to him that I was thinking about taking an early morning newspaper route to supplement my meager sales salary. In an astonished voice, he asked why I would take a paper route when I had a college degree. I told him it was to help pay the rent.

In my brother's opinion, with a college degree, I was supposed to be living the good life and everything was supposed to turn out happily ever after. He was wrong. Even with a college degree, I was broke and working two jobs that I hated.

But that conversation with my brother was a wake-up call, which pulled me out of some depressing thinking. It seemed to snap me out of the hole I was in.

I decided to change my thinking—and I was successful at turning my life around and becoming a millionaire. My success has made me want to show others how they too can be successful.

Success leaves clues.

I thought about the clues I could share, which would show others how to re-think who they are. I thought about how a slight shift or recalculation on their life route could ensure that they end up in a better place.

Deep down, most of us want to be better than we are right now. The problem is that we don't know how to get there. We are oftentimes clueless when we attempt to learn how to make a better life for ourselves.

After what I have learned on my journey, I think it is not such a mystery after all. We just have to be open and willing to change.

4

WHAT IS AN UNLIKELY MILLIONAIRE?

An unlikely millionaire is an average person with average intelligence and few financial resources, who has the courage to break the bonds of working as an employee, and who starts his or her own business in order to become a financial success.

However, it also goes a little farther than that. An unlikely millionaire is someone who appears to have the odds of success stacked against him/her, but perseveres until achieving success.

These people do not have the backing of a rich uncle, or the inside contacts that come from knowing the right people. Unlikely millionaires create their fortune and happiness out of thin air. Despite having the odds seriously stacked against them, they manage to succeed, often to their own surprise.

I am certainly not the first to do it. Many have come before me, and many will come after me. I want you to be one of them.

This is not about being lucky—unless you define lucky as making your own luck. One of my favorite quotes is from Earl Nightingale, who paraphrased the Roman philosopher Seneca the Younger, "Luck is what happens when preparedness and hard work meet opportunity."

Many people have a most unlikely millionaire inside them, just waiting for the opportunity to be released. They are dormant until the programming changes, and it creates a different mindset.

Those destined to become unlikely millionaires do have a few traits in common:

- They have a unique way of thinking that sees the positive in almost every situation. When adversity stands in their way, they either move it out of the way or go around it. They do not allow adversity to prevent them from moving forward.

- They have a curiosity that knows no bounds. When they hear that something cannot be done, it inspires them to find a way to get it done.

- Unlikely millionaires are not afraid of change. In fact, they often embrace change. They see change as a way of differentiating their business from their competitors. They do not go into business to sell the same mousetrap as others are selling. They go into business to sell a better mousetrap.

- They see life as a journey instead of a daily grind. When they are puzzled by something, their first reaction is to learn everything they can about the problem, with a determination to solve it.

When you are willing to grasp life fully by the horns and change your thinking in line with these traits, you too can become an unlikely millionaire.

It was a change in thinking that made me an unlikely millionaire. As I already explained, I did not have ideal teenage years. It was during my college years that I discovered the great inspirational teacher, Earl Nightingale. Studying his lessons helped me change the way I thought about myself and my life.

I came to realize that no one else was going to make my life better. Either I could suffer a lifetime of self-doubt and make feeble attempts at being happy, or I could start to build the life I deserved. I soon began to take action. I started making decisions that separated me from others.

I also took inspiration from the hundreds of thousands of immigrants who came to this country with nothing more than a few dollars in their pockets. They were your ancestors, and mine. Many arrived in this country with nothing but a dream, and they beat the odds to become financially successful. They are all unlikely millionaires.

In addition to Earl Nightingale and hard-working immigrants, I had another inspiration that changed my way of thinking. Although I had my own apartment, I also belonged to a college fraternity. You see, I really was changing. I stopped my habit of shunning other people, and I began seeking out and enjoying the company of others. I was still shy, but I was working on it. I knew I needed to change this part of my personality if I was ever to be successful.

I saw my fraternity brothers graduate and start their careers. I watched as some went to work as employees, while others immediately started their own businesses. Perhaps several of the entrepreneurs got a helping hand from parents or rich relatives, but I didn't pay attention to that at the time.

However, I did pay attention to which of my brothers were becoming the most successful. Those who were employees complained more. They complained about low starting salaries and mundane, entry-level jobs.

Those who started their own businesses were different—very different. Yes, they admitted to me that they were not making much money in the beginning. However, they talked about the money they expected to earn once their businesses began to prosper.

They talked about the challenges of starting a new business. They talked about the challenges of finding solutions to real problems.

And they did talk. Their business was usually their favorite subject to talk about, unlike the guys who were employees, and who mostly talked negatively about their bosses and the companies they worked for.

At the time, I had no idea that I could become that successful, but I admired those who were trying.

I listened to Earl Nightingale's audios regularly. Earl had started his career with the same curiosity about what made some men successful when others were not. As it turned out, Earl earned his own fortune when he had a little nub of an idea—he figured out how to take an existing product and make it better.

At the time, most motivational materials were in the form of books or seminars. Earl's "better mousetrap" was to record his motivational speeches on cassette tapes, and then his customers could listen whenever they wanted.

Earl had a matter-of-fact way of revealing to me that maybe I was the one holding myself back. Maybe what I thought and believed about myself was having a huge negative impact on my life. I listened to those cassette tapes, and later the CDs, for years before I realized that he was right.

5

COULD YOU BE AN UNLIKELY MILLIONAIRE?

Why do so many people think becoming a millionaire is for other people and not for themselves?

What do you think when a BMW or Mercedes speeds by? Do you catch yourself thinking that you could never afford such a fancy car?

What do you think of people who "have it all" (whatever *all* means to you)?

Do you think rich people are smarter, are born with money, or are luckier than you?

If those are your thoughts, you would be wrong at least half of the time.

Granted, some millionaires are born into money, and others are highly intelligent. However, the majority have neither advantage.

A study of 1,300 millionaires revealed that they averaged Cs and Bs in college. Most were not considered great intellectuals.

The fact is that it is your choice to achieve or not to achieve everything that you are capable of. The person who holds you back is the person you see in the mirror every morning.

Always keep in mind that the way you think has a tremendous effect on your life. It is your decision to think in a way that makes you productive, or in a way which has negative consequences to your life.

Consider these two thoughts:

It is another early Monday morning, and I have to drag myself down to the shop to start another workweek.

It is great getting a jumpstart this Monday morning. Getting to the shop early means I can be more productive today.

Which thought do you think will result in a more productive person? Not just for Monday, but for the entire week. I think it is clear that the second thought is the one you need if you want to succeed in life.

It is profound how our thoughts and beliefs either allow us to grow and prosper, or keep us where we are by not allowing us to see the possibilities that are waiting—sometimes just beyond our grasp.

Are you even aware whether your thoughts are predominantly positive or negative? If they are usually negative, have you tried to change them?

If your thoughts are mostly negative, it is time that you consider how they affect the quality of your life. You do not want your thoughts to hold you back.

Slow down for a day or two and consider what you think when you have to make decisions, and when you are being critical of another person or situation. Also consider the meaning of your thoughts.

For example:

- I do not want to get wet in the rain today.
- I want to stay dry today.

Both mean essentially the same thing… or do they?

If you go with the first thought, you are more likely to get wet and grumble about it all day; putting yourself in a bad mood for the day.

By having the second thought, you are more likely to use an umbrella or find another way to stay dry. You are more likely to have a much better day. Why not take a chance by turning your way of thinking around and work toward your dreams?

Who put the notion in your head that you could not be a millionaire? Do you think the neighborhood or family that you grew up in had an influence on your prosperity thinking?

What needs to happen to change your life? Would it be a near-death experience? Would you have to win the lottery?

On the other hand, maybe you believe that you don't have time to make changes. Everyday life is too stressful, and maybe you have no hope that things can be different.

If you are like many people, you are busy with the kids, and your job has you working so many hours that you are just trying to hang on to make ends meet—both financially and emotionally.

Here is an important concept that most people never consider: Are you busy doing the things that are important in your life—or are you simply busy doing those things that are urgent?

The two can be very different.

An example of what is important is something that will change your life for the better. An example of what is urgent could be the deliveryman ringing your doorbell. If I had to choose, I would let the deliveryman leave the package on the porch while I worked at making my life better.

Does that make sense?

Most people are so busy doing what is urgent that they never get around to doing what is important. Not surprisingly, what is urgent often benefits others rather than yourself. If your excuse for not becoming successful is that you are too busy, I want you to start making sure you are doing what is important and tuning out much of what only seems urgent.

Begin each day by making a short list. There should be three categories:

- Urgent and important

- Important

- Urgent but not important

I think you know what to do with that list. Refer to it a few times during the day to make sure the important things are getting done. Start by taking pauses throughout the day to monitor the way you are thinking and make any adjustments as required.

Another part of the urgent confusion is feeling like you are getting a lot done. You might be—but who is benefiting from all of your hard work? If most of your effort is benefiting someone other than yourself and your family, you need to reconsider whether you want to continue down that path. Also, consider if all that busy work is making you happy. When you start looking at some of these things differently, it might motivate you to make positive changes in your life.

Consider how I managed to write a book while raising four children and running a growing business. You wouldn't think I had time to write.

The way I managed it was by getting up a little earlier. The house is quiet between 5:00 a.m. and 7:00 a.m., which is when I found time to write. I also used other opportunities, such as when I was waiting at the airport before flying to various business destinations.

It becomes a matter of making the most out of what time you *do* have. We all get twenty-four hours each day. Use your time to improve your life.

I hope you can see that making a few small changes can result in a profound improvement in your life. Hopefully, you are beginning to understand that the changes are not that big. With a little tweak here and a little tweak there in your thinking, you can become a highly prosperous and very happy person.

Certainly, if I can do it, you can do it. I was not born with a silver spoon in my mouth. Many of my college grades were downright dismal. I just went out and did it—and now it is my mission to show you how you can do it, too.

I am sharing my story because it might be easier for you to believe that you can achieve your dreams if you read about someone just like you (me) who has achieved their dream. To have a role model you can identify with is helpful.

Ask yourself, is life just happening to you or are you making life happen? There is an enormous difference.

Think of your life as a stage play. Someone has to write the script and direct the actors. Most people let someone else (their boss) write the script and direct the play. If you do the same, you have little or no control over your life. Your boss tells you where to stand on the stage and gives you the lines to speak. You are more like a puppet than like a person who is leading his or her own life. You jump when your boss shouts, "Action!" You exit the stage when your boss says, "Change scenes."

You need to be the director of your life. You want to be the one who decides to open and shut the curtain on each act. The director's name is the one that appears first in the playbill. Your name should be at the top, instead of being listed as a stand-in in your own life.

Life is a series of decisions.

Failures are nothing more than opportunities to learn how to make better decisions going forward. The most important lesson to learn is to make your own decisions instead of letting others make them for you.

Most people do not take full responsibility for their own lives. Most go from their parents' control to letting a boss control them.

I encourage you to regress back into childhood to regain your dreams and direction in life. Many times, you will discover your strengths by remembering what you liked to do best when you were a child. Did you like math, writing, or both? Did you like art, science, or sports? What areas of school and what activities did you tend to gravitate towards while you found your passions and special gifts?

The things you loved and what you excelled at as a child and adolescent can give great clues to what makes the most sense for you to do as an adult.

Think about the all too common midlife crisis. This is a time of life when people come to grips with the fact that they are not living the life they want. They are in a rut. In desperation, they start making changes. The classic image of a man having a midlife crisis has him buying the sports car he always wanted as a young man.

Did you know that the Chinese symbol for crisis consists of two characters, one signifying danger, and the other opportunity? How about taking the opportunity inherent in a crisis to become the next most unlikely millionaire?

If I had not experienced it myself, I would find it difficult to believe that an average, middle-aged man could start his own company and live the life of his dreams. It surprised my parents, my family, and me.

Instead of having a midlife crisis, I encourage you to create your "midlife vision" as an unlikely millionaire.

Remember, my transformation into an unlikely millionaire began when I transformed my thinking to believe that I had the power to be anything I wanted. What I wanted most was to be fully in charge of my life, and that meant becoming my own boss by owning my own company. That is the kind of midlife crisis I hope that you have.

I am happy and grateful that I did not remain stuck in my earlier ways of thinking and behaving, since changing my outlook and learning new ways of thinking enabled me to transform my life.

For one reason or another, many people remain stuck for most or all of their lives, thinking that nothing can be different. I hope that by reading my story and the lessons I share, you will want to explore new beliefs about what is possible for you.

Think of the immigrants who came to this country and had nothing but a dream for a better life. They ONLY saw opportunity. Failure was not an option. They left their homeland and decided to build a new life. They had no choice but to succeed.

Think like an immigrant.

Oftentimes, people who were born in the USA take things for granted. Here, anything is possible. You can be anything you want to be. Decide what you want to do and go for it, without looking back.

You must get to a point where you want to change, and BELIEVE that your life can change.

At that junction, an inspirational story can sometimes trigger exploring life in a completely new way with new results. I am hopeful that my true story and the lessons I learned will be the spark that wakes up new desires in you for positive change in your life.

6

WHAT WE CAN LEARN FROM CHILDREN

Are you smarter than a fifth grader?

In my opinion, many children are smarter than most adults are. Children are definitely smarter than we give them credit for.

Children prove that we are all born with natural talents and abilities. Each of us was born with the certainty and confidence that anything is possible. After we become adults, we begin to believe that we have limitations. We stop believing that we can be anything we want to be.

As a father of two boys and two girls, ages twelve, ten, eight, and five, I have witnessed how amazing children are. They are full of ability and talent, and see life as an endless possibility.

From my own children, I have seen firsthand the unlimited amounts of energy, faith, and confidence they have. It is a spirit that anything is possible and achievable if we put our minds to what we want.

Unlimited possibility and the ability to achieve anything is one of the most important lessons we can learn from children.

Ask yourself, "What do I really want from life?" Answering that question opens a new horizon of lifestyle choices. Children remind us that boundaries are self-created and self-enforced. As adults, we build invisible boundaries about what we can achieve. These false boundaries soon become our truth and create lines we can no longer cross.

At an early age, my oldest son, Antonio, demonstrated his determination to achieve goals. He was so determined to walk that he was willing to fall down again and again. Even after cracking his head and getting stitches in his forehead twice, he persevered. Nothing was going to stop him from achieving his goal of walking, not even pain and two visits to the hospital!

Antonio is a perfect example of the idea that each of us was born with sheer determination to try new things and persist, over and over, until we reach our goals. As adults, we lose this pigheaded stick-to-itiveness, courage, and willingness to go for what we want. I am sure you are like Antonio, i.e., you fell many times while learning to walk. And as a small child, you persevered. As adults, we come to believe that the probability of failure outweighs the possibility of success—once we fail at something, we should give up. We are sometimes scared to take a risk and possibly fail. Better to do nothing at all than to be considered a failure. But that is not the way to success.

My five-year-old daughter, Francesca (we call her Freshie), wakes up every day with a big smile. She is always excited about what the new day has in store for her. She sees each day as an adventure.

I've seen Freshie go to bed, all scraped, and bruised after taking a bike fall. It makes no difference—the next day, she bounces out of bed with a smile, and is ready to try the bike again.

As adults, what can we learn from Freshie's attitude toward life? Of course, we have bills to pay and are exposed to more stressful situations than a child is, but we still have a choice in how we respond to our daily lives.

At any given moment, whether it is the first thing in the morning or right after a stressful event, you have a choice of how to respond and think about events.

You can go at it relaxed and confident that everything will be fine (because this is usually true). Or you can pile self-pity onto an already stressful day.

Children believe anything is possible. As an adult, do you think anything is possible? Is your career or job really what you want it to be? Are you pursuing your dreams and passions?

From an early age, children begin to dream and think that anything is possible for them. Whatever they can dream up or draw with a crayon becomes reality. They easily see themselves as astronauts, dancers, and football stars.

Who is living in the real reality—the adult or the child?

Interesting question.

My daughter Isabella started watching cooking shows at the age of six. Almost immediately, she wanted to open her own restaurant—Isabella's Café. My wife and I were a little surprised that our six-year-old kid insisted on watching cooking shows and helping mom in the kitchen instead of being glued to cartoons and Dora the Explorer.

At age twelve, she is still watching cooking shows and is 100% convinced that one day soon she will open Isabella's Café and become a famous chef. Cooking is her passion and she wants it to become her career.

How many adults discover their natural calling and then commit enough courage and energy to go after what they want? They usually give in and get a job just to make money and live their lives in quiet desperation. Something to ponder...

The fact is there are no valid reasons or obstacles preventing you from dreaming like a child. You truly just need to decide that you want to think, just as children do. It can be both fun and rewarding to live life through the lessons and eyes of a child.

Beyond the fact that children find everything to be possible in this world, they also develop their natural talents early in life. Everyone is born with natural talents, and the trick is not to be put into a box with everyone else.

Some children learn early that they can carry a tune and sing better than other children. Others are academically inclined and excel at math, science, and reading.

Math did not come naturally to me as a child, nor as an adult. Because I know this, I never pursued a career that required me to use a lot of math. In fact, I avoid it like the plague—no reason to stress myself out.

Children learn early whether they are predominantly right-brain, left-brain, or a combination of both. This fact reveals itself from experiences when we learn our strengths and weaknesses.

Do you know which you are? Think back to what you excelled at as a child. This will give you a big clue about what you are better suited to be doing as an adult. It could be that discovering the answer to this will lead you to becoming an unlikely millionaire.

Another common quality of young children is that they ask for what they want, over and over and over. It isn't unusual for one of my kids to ask thirty-two times, "Can I have that toy?" Children focus on what they want—and they do not easily or quickly take *no* for an answer.

As children grow older, they are taught by adults that they can't have everything they want. As they grow, children are taught by adults not to ask for what they want, and they are taught to avoid trying something new for fear of failure.

Of course, every child is unique; this is obvious in my own children. They do not have the same passions. One of my boys is great at sports and loves it. The other does not like sports as much. Two of my kids love reading everything they can get their hands on. My oldest daughter does not enjoy reading.

We are all different, we are all unique, and we all have special gifts.

As adults, we rarely try new things. We get in the same groove because we have programmed ourselves to believe we cannot do anything else.

What is interesting about children is that they will explore and try almost anything. They will play soccer. They will try wrestling. They will try any sport to see if they are good at it, and to see whether they will find it fun.

My wife and I constantly expose our children to different things, such as tae kwon do. We have three black belts in the house.

My oldest daughter loves playing volleyball. We only discovered that after she tried six other sports.

My oldest son, Antonio, is not into team sports, but he is a black belt in tae kwon do. He also loves going to museums. He is an artist, and he has won several awards for his work.

My next boy, Lorenzo, who is eight, does not like art much. Instead, he plays every team sport there is, from basketball to football. He practices tae kwon do as well. He thrives in a competitive environment, whereas Antonio does not.

We all thrive, grow, learn, and develop in our own way—and that is good. We are individuals with different passions and talents. Society seems to group everyone together, and makes outcasts of those who are brave enough to claim their uniqueness.

The point of this chapter is that we sometimes get lost as adults. We get a job to make money rather than finding our passion and aligning a job with our passion.

More than likely, you are one of the millions of people who are simply getting by—working in a job that is not fulfilling.

The better aligned your profession is to your natural gifts and abilities, the faster you will become successful and the happier you will be.

The trick is to re-discover your childlike passion, which knows no boundaries. As adults, we sometimes get overwhelmed with life and forget the wonders and possibilities that life has to offer.

Find that childlike passion again. Bring that fearless inner-child out and have the courage to know that anything is possible if you believe.

Let us be inspired by the youngster described below:

A kindergarten teacher gave an assignment for the students to draw a picture of anything they wanted to draw. She looked over the shoulder of one little girl and asked her what she was drawing.

The little girl replied, "I am drawing a picture of God."

The teacher responded, "No one knows what God looks like."

The little girl looked up at the teacher and said, "They will in a minute."

7

THE IMPORTANCE OF HABITS

I t might surprise you how many of your thoughts, behaviors, and actions are the same today as the day before, and the day before, and the day before.

In other words, you are probably not even aware that "habits" have been putting you in an auto-pilot state for most of your life. If you don't recognize that your habits command much of your time, it is more challenging to change or modify them.

Habits can work for you or against you, and it would be beneficial to identify and keep those that are productive, and discard those that hold you back.

It is easy to let habitual behavior drive you like a software program on a computer. How do you like your programming? Is it working in your life? Perhaps it would be helpful to write some new codes and commands.

Habits put people in a somewhat automatic, robotic mode, and most people, most of the time, do not realize this is happening. Habits control days; days turn into weeks; weeks into months; months into years; years into decades. You do things without even thinking about it... even things that will kill you.

A clear example of a habit that does not work is cigarette smoking. Forget for a moment that cigarettes are addictive. I am talking just about the habitual behavior. Typically, smoking cigarettes starts out innocently. We say to ourselves, "Hey, it's just one cigarette..." And then one turns to two, and two into half a pack a day, and so on.

After one or two cigarettes our health is not obviously impacted much—but as smoking becomes a habit, those first few cigarettes can turn into multiple years (or even decades) of smoking. At that point, we have a full-blown habit that is difficult to break and which will negatively impact all areas of our lives and oftentimes have lethal health consequences.

However, habits of thinking poorly about ourselves are not as obvious as this example. Nonetheless, these negative habits can be just as lethal to our enjoyment of life and to what we can accomplish. These habits are not as obviously unhealthy as smoking—the impact of bad thinking habits is hidden and harmful, which makes them very dangerous.

Why not lift the fog off these habits, in all areas of our lives, and decide which habits we want to change?

Why do we eat food that we know is not good for our bodies? We find ourselves driving through the local fast-food restaurant because it's quick and easy, with no real thought behind the consequences.

How are we doing with exercise? Do we pack our bags and drive to the gym three days a week, like we have promised others and ourselves, or does something always come up that seems more important and somehow it doesn't seem to happen as planned?

Maybe we love exercise and how we feel after a great workout, so we do whatever it takes to get in thirty or forty minutes per day—in this case, it is a habit that works in our favor, not against us.

Some of the more challenging habits to identify, and decide if they are beneficial, are habits of thought and habits of behavior. These are not so obvious and can be elusive.

What are your daily thought habits?

What are your daily habits for enjoying life?

What are your daily habits for complaining?

Whether we're conscious of it or not, we are following our habits day in and day out. We develop routines for everything from what time we wake up, to how we brush our teeth. Do you start brushing your teeth on your right side or left side? Are you paying attention to how you put on your shoes and socks? Are you putting on sock-sock-shoe-shoe or do you put on sock-shoe-sock-shoe?

My message in this chapter is this; realize that habits drive your life. Regardless of whether they are good or bad habits, they control almost every aspect of your life.

You need to be aware of your habits. Some habits, like exercising every day, are productive and healthy. Others are unhealthy.

Because you might not see the results of bad habits for many years, you need to stop them now.

One of the biggest habits to evaluate is the way you think. This was a game changer for me, to realize that my thinking was not productive. I still struggle with it—I still catch myself going down the rat hole.

What I am trying to say is to be aware of what is going on. If you find yourself with a habit of negative thinking, there are ways to change. The easiest way to change a habit is to replace it with something else, instead of just stopping it.

My negative thinking lasted until I was twenty-two years old. I didn't think I was good enough. I didn't think I was smart enough. I didn't think I could ever be successful. That was my habit of thought for twenty-two years. It was not until I discovered the teachings of Earl Nightingale that I started to change my thinking. And that was a big deal for me.

Habits of thought and behavior are some of the more challenging to identify. You must decide if they are beneficial to you or not. These effects are less obvious and can be elusive to pinpoint. However, making changes in how you think and behave can be very valuable to your happiness and wealth.

Most people are fully aware of their eating, drinking, and exercise habits. However, their habits of thought are rarely considered.

What you need to do right now is hit that pause button and take the time to consider whether you are enjoying life to the fullest. Assuming that you are not, (otherwise why would you be reading this book?) what are you going to change so that you can enjoy life to the fullest?

There will never be a better time for this life-changing mental exercise than right now. No one can make better changes to the quality of your life than you. It is your life and your choice. You have the freedom and ability to choose which habits you embrace and which ones you stop.

When you start your morning by thinking that it is going to be a rotten day, it will be a rotten day. You will make sure of it. When you start your morning thinking that it will be a joyful day, it will be a joyful day.

Make it your habit to experience every moment of every day with a happy and grateful spirit.

If you constantly find yourself in the company of people who bring you down, you can choose to avoid them. Instead of hanging out with the negative people, put yourself in the company of people who bring happiness to your life.

Remember, the easiest way to break a bad habit is to replace it with a good habit. If you find yourself frequently entertaining a negative view of yourself, or of the world around you, make a conscious effort to find the good in both the world and yourself. Replace your negative thoughts with positive thoughts and make positive thinking your new habit.

If you are too busy reacting to what is going on in your life, it is because that is how you choose to live. Your life will never get better until you take the time to hit the pause button and make the changes that need to be made.

You have one life to live, so enjoy it on your terms.

8

RISK VS. SECURITY

Some people think that it is risky to create their own business, and that they are secure when they work for someone else. I disagree. I believe that running your own business is often a more stable and rewarding way to make a living while having long-term control over your destiny. Usually it is also more financially rewarding.

Ponder this scenario:

After being laid-off from five different jobs in eight months, John was hired by a company to work in their warehouse. One day, he lost control of the forklift and drove it off the loading dock.

Looking over the damage, the owner shook his head and said, "I am sorry, John, but I am going to have to withhold 5% of your wages until the damage is paid for."

"How much will it cost?" John asked.

"I estimate ten thousand dollars," the owner replied.

"What a relief!" John replied. "Finally, I have job security."

All kidding aside, job security has become a scarce commodity. It is no longer like the 1960s and 1970s, when you worked for the same company for thirty years and then retired with a gold watch and a decent pension.

Almost every child is taught that they are supposed to get good grades in school, go to college, and then get a well-paying job with a company that is healthy and growing.

For some, that route in life can be fulfilling and rewarding. Others realize that getting a job and working for someone else is more risky than starting their own business and controlling their own destiny.

We learned this lesson from the Great Recession of 2008, when millions of unfortunate workers discovered that their jobs were not as secure as they thought.

In most big corporations, there is little employee loyalty. The bosses answer to a board of directors, and ultimately to the shareholders, not the workers who create the revenue. Almost every employee in any major corporation is attempting to build a career on a loose and shaky foundation.

Sadly, many people thought they had job security. Because of that false sense of security, they had not bothered to learn any other skills which would allow them to adapt to a new career or to find other ways of earning income. They were a small cog in a big machine, with specialized skills that didn't apply anywhere else.

You are likely to have more control and real security when you take a calculated, intelligent risk by striking out on your own to serve others in the marketplace. When times get tough, you will have many more options to adjust and adapt your business by changing products, changing strategies, cutting costs, etc.

Not only tough economic times can erase a job. Often when two companies merge into one, it means that the mega-corporation must get rid of extra employees. Improved technology has also resulted in the loss of jobs when humans are replaced by automation. Even if any of these situations doesn't occur, managers are always looking for ways to streamline the business, and your position could be the one on the chopping block.

Most people are looking for income security in the wrong places. Statistics show that 91% of people entering the job/ business market for the first time are focused on working for someone else. That leaves only 9% who want to start their own business.

Imagine the talk at unemployment offices and among graduating college students. Most are probably saying, "If I could only get a job, I would be happy and everything will be okay." This way of thinking comes from years of false programming.

I tell my children (and anyone else who will listen) to ask themselves, "What kind of business can I start that would serve the marketplace in a unique way? What are the needs of the marketplace, and what possibilities are available?"

Starting a business goes far beyond having more security than you could get from working for someone else. In many cases, it pays much better. Depending on the type of business, during the early startup years the income is typically not great, but over the long haul, the earnings can make you wealthy.

This line of thinking is not for the short-term, career-minded individual. It is better suited for someone who wants to have control over his or her future, finances, and the life they create for their family.

In my case, I took a significant cut in pay for several years while working harder than ever, both physically and mentally. But, as I look back twenty years later, I am extremely grateful and happy that I decided to do what I did.

Granted, some years have been financially better than others. In the good years, we traveled quite a bit. When times got tough, we made adjustments—but we were still okay, and no one was out of a job or a paycheck.

Another aspect of taking an intelligent risk by starting a business is that you might end up surprising yourself, and become more successful than you anticipated. For example, when I first started my business, I had a burning desire to strike out on my own. I wanted to prove to myself and to others

(I think it might have been my dad) that I could do something great.

In the early years, I did not have dreams of incredible success for my business. I just wanted something I could call my own, even if it was small. I did want to be able to live off the profits eventually, but money was not the driver for me. I wanted to have control and to prove the point that I could do something more with my life.

Don't be afraid of failing. You will discover what works and what doesn't. I tried different things. My first business was a real-estate development company that I started when I was around twenty-five years old. The business only survived eighteen months, and I lost $10,000 of my hard-earned money.

There is no failure, only feedback. I got the feedback I needed and proceeded to start a marketing company where we created promotions and ads for car dealerships. That only lasted one year. However, I got the feedback I needed.

I learned that I needed to quit my full-time job and give my all to the business. I always had one foot in and one foot out. I needed to be committed to my business. In addition, I needed to have the courage to go out on a limb, try something new, and then take action.

Well, the third time was the charm. With the help of incredible people, such as my business partner and other strategic partners, the business grew and became successful in several ways. I was pleasantly surprised that we were able to transform a startup label business—which was started with two partners each contributing $15,000 that we borrowed from credit cards—into a remarkable business with stellar employees and many happy, well-paying customers. My point is this—starting a business can be an awakening of what you can actually accomplish, and you just might surprise yourself. You only have to take action, and not let fear of failure stop you, as it has done to so many others.

Some mornings, while I am walking up to our two big business buildings, I think to myself, "Jeez, look at this! We are doing well for two guys who didn't know what they were doing in the beginning."

Starting a business can be an enlightening growth experience and it can evolve into a great success—but this will never be possible if you are not willing to take a calculated risk. There may be a winner in that new business you always wanted to start.

In contrast, let's take a look at the I-need-to-get-a-job strategy. For the majority of people, an entry-level position ends up becoming a ten-year or thirty-year job. For example, how many people do you know who start working somewhere, just to get a job, and end up staying with the same employer much longer than they imagined? They don't seem to be able to venture out and look for other jobs or other career options. For these people, the "surprises" in terms of success and financial security are minimal. They are playing it safe; betting on what they think is a sure thing.

For most employees, an annual-cost-of-living raise and a Christmas bonus are the only ways to earn more money—which limits lifestyle options for them and their families. Before they know it, twenty-two years have passed, and at that point, they might think it is too late to change careers.

The Great Recession of 2008 showed us that there is no job security. You are better off striking out on your own. The downsizing, merging, and changing marketplace are now called the New Economy. You can have special skills and offer a great contribution to your employer—but that still might not be enough when the next round of layoffs comes.

Even if you have a job, don't let yourself be lulled into thinking that everything is great. I have a talented friend who worked for a medical device company. That is one of the most solid and successful industries today.

He sold medical devices for about seven years, and he was the company's top salesperson. Out of left field, and unknown to him, there was a merger. A larger company bought the company that he worked for. One of the first changes the company made after the merger was to consolidate the sales force. When I next talked with my friend, he said, "I'm out of a job, Eric. I can't believe it." In his mind, being the top salesperson gave him job security.

In reality, his job security was part of the grand illusion.

When you work for yourself, you have full control of your business. You control the hours, you control the investment, and you control the opportunities. You decide what direction your business heads in. You decide when your business needs any changes—changes to survive an economic downturn or changes that increase revenue and profits. There is much security in being at the helm. With your own business, you control your destiny— you are writing your own paychecks—and with that comes peace of mind and a feeling of power.

9

WHY BE NORMAL?

I f you decide you want to improve your life by going into business for yourself, there are a few different ways of doing it.

The Small Business Administration and SCORE offer free
advice and guidance for new business owners. They are both
good resources when beginning a new business.

Regardless of the type of business that you decide on, you
have a critical decision at the beginning—how do you want to be
positioned in the marketplace?

Many of the people who start a business soon fail, because all
they did was copy the way another successful business operated.
This logic can work if you purchase a franchise and the franchisor
limits the number of stores that operate in your geographical
area.

You can also start a business that is similar to others in your marketplace if there is a large enough market to support more than one. In fact, often the most successful businesses are in underserviced sectors of the market.

When opening a business that is similar to several others in the marketplace, there is one significant step to take. You need to have your own unique and important twist to the business. It might not be the easiest thing to do at the beginning—to make a plan to both survive and be unique—but being different is a phenomenal short-term and long-term strategy to make sure your new business thrives.

Why be normal when you can be different?

Some entrepreneurs make the mistake of thinking that they can sell a brand-new product or service to create a market that does not yet exist. Seldom does this strategy work.

You need an existing market to start a business. One example I am familiar with is Atari, the electronic game company. When it was established in 1971, Atari was ahead of its time since there was not yet an established market for electronic games. Atari struggled for several years before finally going belly up. It could not establish a large enough market to become profitable. Today, Nintendo, Sony, and Microsoft make billions in an established electronic game market.

The key point is—a small business cannot create a market. A better strategy is to find an under-served market and bring something unique to it that adds value for customers.

In business, finding and keeping customers and making a profit is easier if your product or service is somehow different or unique from what your competitors offer, but not so unique that you will have to educate consumers.

I had success starting a business eighteen years ago. The business had steady growth for ten years. Then, as the company matured, the business ran out of steam, the competition became stronger, and profit margins began to shrink. When a company is not growing and margins are shrinking, you can only cut costs so much before real problems start to occur. If a change or reinvention of the business does not happen, the firm will eventually go out of business.

At the ten-year mark, my business partner and I discovered a book by W. Chan Kim and Renee Mauborgne titled Blue Ocean Strategy. What we learned from that one book saved our business. Implementing this one strategy helped us breathe new life into the dying business.

The blue ocean strategy is a different way of creating and operating a business. For example, when done correctly, a business with a blue ocean strategy views itself as a boat all alone on a vast blue ocean. Doing business in the blue ocean means "creating" new market space for a business, instead of "competing" for new market space like everyone else. The blue ocean strategy is a unique way of serving customers in a marketplace that didn't exist before.

The opposite (typically normal business model) is what the authors called the red ocean, which means your competition is selling similar products to similar consumers or businesses at similar prices.

Profit margins become squeezed and it can be challenging to add value to the marketplace. So when considering going into business, it is critical to decide whether you want to hang out in a blue ocean or a red ocean.

Let me give you two examples of the blue ocean strategy. One is from the book, Blue Ocean Strategy, and the other is from personal experience.

In the book, the authors give an example that most people can relate to... Cirque du Soleil. Cirque du Soleil is an entertainment experience created in the past fifteen years, and the creation of this entertainment experience uses the blue ocean strategy. A red ocean strategy would be if they copied the Barnum and Bailey Circus acts, which have been performed for over a hundred years. What the creator of Cirque du Soleil did differently was to borrow elements from the traditional Barnum and Bailey Circus and elements of the show experience from the traditional theatre, like Broadway plays, and blend them into a unique (not competitive) new market space. Cirque du Soleil is a different and powerful entertainment experience that does not have any similar competition, at least for now. They are the pioneers, and so they will enjoy a dominant market share, assuming that they continue their journey of growth and success.

You might think the Cirque du Soleil example conflicts with my previous comments about not being able to create a marketplace where one does not exist. Let me clarify. In the Cirque du Soleil example, a marketplace existed. Cirque du Soleil brought a completely new and unique experience to an existing market.

When my partner and I started our business in 2003, we did the normal business strategy of playing copycat by creating a business model similar to what we already knew. We would buy a product for X amount, mark it up 20% to 30%, and then sell it to our customers. Along the way, we added value and great customer service. This worked for a while.

In our case, our business was selling label-making machines and all the needed supplies, so that manufacturers could print their own shipping and barcode labels in-house. This gave our customers more control and flexibility over the packaging part of their operations. For us, this model worked, and we did pretty well for ten years or so. We started the business in pure survival mode, and then we moved onto the growth phase, then to the maturity period, until the business started to slow down.

We decided to make the bold move to manufacture labels. We decided to shift away from a broker or distribution model. But not only did we want to manufacture labels, we also wanted to manufacture labels in a way that was truly a blue ocean strategy. In other words, we wanted to play the label manufacturing game differently and used blue ocean thinking instead of making labels just like everyone else in the business (red ocean).

To create our blue ocean, we decided first to be different and better at serving our customers. We had to focus on the overlooked wants and needs of our customers. This sounds logical, but the majority of companies build a business and a manufacturing site the traditional way. They build it and then force their customers to buy the products and services the way they want to produce them.

In contrast, we decided to take a new, innovative approach and spend some time exploring and discovering what our customers really wanted from a label-manufacturing company if the boundaries were lifted and anything was possible. We started by letting customers know we had a clean slate. We wanted to position ourselves to serve the existing marketplace in a completely new way.

To our amazement, we discovered that our customers and prospective customers had needs that were not met by anyone servicing the market. This was because no one had ever taken the time or had the forethought to interview the customers and learn how they could be better served.

This is what we did with our blue ocean strategy: We interviewed current and potential customers and discovered they had three critical needs—or three pain points—that were a direct result of the current way labeling companies produced labels.

These needs were:

1. Fixed price per unit instead of variable cost per unit (label).

In the traditional business model for label manufacturing, pricing is based on the concept that the more you buy, the cheaper the price. This leads to variable pricing and forces buyers to oftentimes buy more labels than they really need at a given time. This sounds minor, but when you dig deep, the variable price per label and the requirement to buy more than they wanted did not serve customers very well; especially in tough times like the Recession of 2008.

This way of doing business created excess inventory (business cash flow), obsolete inventory, and wastage (when information on the label changed). Having to pay a variable price for labels is tough when it is important for a business to know its costs and budget, and to be able to make decisions based on real or true costs.

2. Shipping the exact quantity of labels that were ordered.

This sounds so simple, but in traditional models, nearly every label manufacturer shipped 10% more than the customer actually ordered. The reason the manufactures did this was because everyone else did it, and they all chimed in together and said shipping 10% over what was ordered was the "industry standard." Well, receiving 10% more than what was ordered does not serve the customer... it serves the label company. This extra 10% can turn into waste, and in most cases, it is a nightmare for accounting and receiving departments, since they are looking at invoices telling them they ordered 100,000 labels but are now expected to receive and pay for 110,000 labels. Talk to any controller or CFO and he/she will tell you, they don't like this way of doing business.

3.   Delivering the very best quality at the very best price.

Traditionally, in the label business, this is not the case. Something usually suffers, be it lead-time, quality, or price.

We discovered these three needs through our interviews with customers.

With this valuable information, we built a plant and selected equipment, technologies, and processes to satisfy these needs. In doing this, we had the confidence that we could help other businesses by offering them a better way of ordering labels.

After four years of building and expanding our label plant using a blue ocean strategy, we achieved the following:

- We won more awards than any other label company in the USA for quality and innovation by the end of 2011.
- We reported a striking rate of growth in sales and profits in 2011, exceeding 22% growth annually.

- We had a proprietary process and manufacturing facility, which served customers in a unique and beneficial way.

Getting into manufacturing using a blue ocean approach was the turning point, even though the first two years were tough—which should be expected by anyone starting a new business. The first six to twenty-four months are definitely going to be the toughest part of your new journey.

It is like the movie Field of Dreams with Kevin Costner. Sometimes if you build it, they will come. So we built it, and though they did not come right away, eventually they did come.

Many people give up much too early. I hope that you do not. You just have to realize that you'll need some kind of financial means to hang in there for at least for six months.

Starting your own business is not a source of instant financial gratification. It is an investment and it takes a long-term strategy to become successful. You just have to realize this and keep reminding yourself at the beginning that growing a business is like planting a tree. You plant it, you fertilize it, and you nurture it. The fruit might not come for two to four years—but when it does come you will have more fruit than you ever thought possible.

Moreover, if you use the blue ocean strategy, you will be way ahead of the game. Before you start your business, make a raw business plan, and then tweak it when you get feedback. Interview customers in your niche to find out how you can serve them better. Find out what your competition is doing wrong, and then do it right. It is important to differentiate yourself from the crowd. If you can deliver your products or services in a unique way, you are more likely to be a success.

10

ACHIEVE BALANCE BEFORE IT'S TOO LATE

E ntrepreneurs have a tendency to throw themselves into their work. They go all in. But, as I discussed in the first part of the book, life is really about happiness and doing what you want. You have to create balance in your life to be truly happy.

Many average people have successfully started their own businesses, and there are those who have become successful behind a corporate desk.

People work hard because that is what they are programmed to do—it seems to be the right thing to do. However, sometimes we work to the point of damaging our health and/or our relationships. The price paid is not worth the return.

I have done it myself. About six years ago, I was working such long hours that it was affecting my health, and it was impacting my family.

With a big family and a successful business, there have been times when I get so caught up in rushing that I miss out on what is going on around me. There was one day, for some reason I had slowed down, just for a moment. I was walking my daughter to school; she was five at the time, and I decided to really enjoy the moment. It sounds so simple, but I was holding her hand while we were walking. She was smiling. I was smiling. It was only about a four-minute walk, but I was fully in the moment and it felt so right. I knew my daughter appreciated it, and it made me feel like I was doing something right as a father.

Just then, a man ran past us, pulling his child behind him—literally hanging onto the pinky finger of the child. I thought, "That guy is really missing out." Truth is, I know that I had been like that guy more times than not.

We all need a balanced life; setting a balance between work, relationships, family, and health.

We have all heard stories of successful businesspersons who work to the detriment of their health. They might be overweight from bad eating habits, or have other health issues.

Here is an example I am familiar with: A loan officer was over-working year after year. One day, he had a mild heart attack. That's what it took for him to realize that he was out of balance and needed to take time to take care of himself and his family. A heart attack is a serious signpost; a warning signal that cannot be ignored. Why not make a change before that happens?

Working too many hours can be unproductive. Overworking can lead to less productivity than if you took time off to get some rest. Some people do not realize this until they have a health issue or they damage their relationship and go through a divorce.

I have a good friend who is a great lawyer. He has his own firm and he is financially well off. He has good health but he went through a divorce. The divorce process went on for over ten years. During that time, his relationship with his two oldest sons deteriorated. He deeply regrets it. Unfortunately, he cannot get back that lost time. It is gone forever.

On the surface, he appeared to be a success. We tend to think of success in monetary terms—but if you don't have balance between work, family, and play, you will never be among the truly successful.

In the end, money is only money. Money by itself will never make you happy or buy you happiness. Most people derive their happiness from good relationships with family and friends.

There is no point in becoming a millionaire only to wake up one morning and realize that you have no one to share your prosperity with. I am certain that I would prefer far less than a million, and have my family and friends, rather than have millions of dollars and be lonely.

I am proud to say that I have a strong relationship with my wife and all four of our children. None of them thinks that they have had to sacrifice our relationships in exchange for the good life.

In my way of thinking, if I've worked hard for the good life, I want a long life to enjoy what I have created.

At the beginning of this book, I emphasized that you need to be aware of what can happen if there is no balance. I am trying to raise your awareness about this again so that you understand how truly important balance is.

Becoming an unlikely millionaire is as much about total happiness as it is about earning lots of money.

There are people who will tell you that you can only have one or the other; that you must choose your business or your family. That simply is not true. I live a full life that includes both. I believe you will be more productive, have better ideas, and be more creative when you are healthy, happy, and have a great home life. Some of your best ideas and inspirations will come when you have all those pistons firing at once.

If you go about it the right way, and keep the balance, you *will* have it all. Just do it the right way.

CREATING YOUR DREAM LIFE IS EASIER THAN YOU MIGHT THINK

By reading this book, I hope you realize that only you and your thoughts are holding you back from creating your dream life. I also want you to say, "If this guy can do it, I can do it!"

Let's recap...

What You Learned As a Child

When you were six years old, you woke up every day with the thought that anything was possible. You kept asking for what you wanted because you knew if you asked enough times, you were probably going to get it.

- Do not take no for an answer.
- Have the boldness of a child.

- Believe that the world will deliver whatever you ask for.

- Discover what you are good at… what makes you happy.

- Play and laugh and have fun!

That childlike wonder is still inside you. You only have to take time to reflect and rediscover your passion. It is there. It is waiting for you to wake up.

How to Find Your Way Back

You find your way back by hitting the pause button and taking time to examine where you are, what you are thinking, and what is possible.

The truth is, you can do whatever you want to do. Nothing—outside of yourself—is holding you back.

The Importance of Habits

From the time you open your eyes in the morning until the time you go to sleep at night, your actions are being influenced by your habits. Be aware of which habits are working for you and which are not. Then, replace any bad habits with good habits.

The most important habit of all is to be aware of how you think. People have approximately 60,000 thoughts a day. If you can start to monitor and capture which thoughts are working for you and which are not, you are headed in a positive direction, and that is the key to success. It just takes a slight tweak... the smallest change can alter your life in a big way.

Risk vs. Security

Job security is an illusion. In today's world, starting your own business is less risky than taking a job and working for somebody else.

There has never been a better time to start your own business.

Of course, it would be wise to create a business plan and seek out assistance from SCORE or the Small Business Administration.

You can do it.

Starting Your Own Business is One of the Best Ways to Become an Unlikely Millionaire

Eighty-five percent of millionaires earned their wealth by owning a business. Getting rich is not as difficult as you might think.

When you are passionate about your business, you are more likely to be successful.

Different is Better

Creating a unique business model is a desirable short-term and long-term strategy. You want to think about establishing a business that is not like any other. You will have a lot more fun and be a lot more successful.

You need to do some groundwork by conducting customer interviews, and doing your homework to make your business stand out from the competition and be seen as unique.

People start businesses that are like every other business in a particular industry and then wonder why they fail. Don't fall into that trap. Do something different. Find out what is not working in other businesses and do the opposite.

Achieve Balance Before It's Too Late

You need to realize that you don't need to sacrifice your family or your health to have a successful business.

It's not all about money. If you have a lot of money, but you are not healthy, or you have no one to share your financial success with, the money is meaningless.

Don't be tricked into believing that if you have money, you will have happiness. There must be a balance. It is possible to have it all.

What is Keeping You From Living Your Dream Life?

The unlikely millionaire is sleeping right there inside you. Use this opportunity to coax it awake. Train your mind to tell you that you can create the life of your dreams. Do not let another day slip by.

Maybe you are waiting for a specific date to make a change. Are you waiting for "someday?" I have seen many calendars and I have never found one that had "someday" on it. Does some-day come after Monday or does someday come once every blue moon?

Choose today to be your someday—the day you make the decision to change your life.

No matter what you have done in the past, you can start fresh today.

I hope that after reading my story, you make life-changing decisions, and that what once seemed impossible to you, now seems possible.

I strongly encourage you to act on what you have learned, so that you too can become a most unlikely millionaire.

For resources, tips, and other tools to help you become the

next most unlikely millionaire, please visit:

www.mostunlikelymillionaire.com

ABOUT THE AUTHOR

Eric Shepard is living the American dream.

After graduating from California State University, Fullerton with a degree in communication, his career path was uncertain. After several failed business endeavors, he overcame personal and professional obstacles to become the co-founder of the multi-million dollar company, Labeltronix.

His belief: if this ordinary, middle class guy, with average intelligence, resources and skills can become a millionaire, anyone can! His calling is to share his secrets to success so that others may also become an unlikely millionaire.

Eric is living the life of his dreams in California, with his wife, Stacie, and their four children, Antonio, Lorenzo, Isabella, and Freshie.

NOTES:

NOTES:

NOTES:

NOTES:

NOTES:

NOTES:

www.ingramcontent.com/pod-product-compliance
Lightning Source LLC
Chambersburg PA
CBHW071528200326
41519CB00019B/6116